PRINCEWILL LAGANG

Understanding Love Languages

First published by PRINCEWILL LAGANG 2023

Copyright © 2023 by Princewill Lagang

All rights reserved. No part of this publication may be reproduced, stored or transmitted in any form or by any means, electronic, mechanical, photocopying, recording, scanning, or otherwise without written permission from the publisher. It is illegal to copy this book, post it to a website, or distribute it by any other means without permission.

Princewill Lagang asserts the moral right to be identified as the author of this work.

First edition

This book was professionally typeset on Reedsy.
Find out more at reedsy.com

Contents

1	Introduction to Love Languages	1
2	The Five Love Languages Unveiled	4
3	Acts of Service: Expressing Love Through Actions	7
4	Words of Affirmation: The Power of Positive Words	10
5	Receiving Gifts: Symbolic Expressions of Love	13
6	Quality Time: The Value of Undivided Attention	16
7	Physical Touch: The Language of Physical Connection	19
8	Discovering Your Partner's Love Language	22
9	Navigating Relationships with Different Love Languages	25
10	Applying Love Languages in Daily Life	28
11	Enhancing Intimacy Through Love Languages	31
12	The Journey of Love Languages	34

1

Introduction to Love Languages

Love Languages and Their Significance

In the intricate landscape of human emotions and relationships, the concept of love languages serves as a profound framework for understanding how individuals express and receive love. Coined by Dr. Gary Chapman in his groundbreaking book "The Five Love Languages," love languages are essentially the distinct ways in which people communicate and interpret love. This concept revolutionized the way we perceive romantic relationships, friendships, and familial bonds.

Dr. Chapman identifies five primary love languages, each representing a unique mode of emotional communication: Words of Affirmation, Acts of Service, Receiving Gifts, Quality Time, and Physical Touch. People tend to have a primary and secondary love language, influencing their preferences in how they both express love and feel loved.

The significance of love languages lies in their power to foster mutual understanding and emotional connection between individuals. Relationships can often encounter difficulties when partners express affection in a way they understand but may not be fully comprehensible to their significant other. By becoming aware of and embracing each other's love languages, individuals can bridge the gap between their intentions and their partner's perception, leading to more fulfilling and harmonious relationships.

Setting the Stage for Exploration

As we embark on this journey to explore the intricate interplay of love languages within relationships, it's crucial to recognize that every individual's emotional makeup is unique. This book aims to delve deep into each of the five love languages, unraveling their essence, and shedding light on how they manifest in various relationships. Through real-life anecdotes, psychological insights, and practical advice, we will navigate the diverse ways in which love languages can influence both the highs and lows of relationships.

Throughout this exploration, we will also uncover how cultural influences, personal experiences, and individual personalities contribute to the formation of one's love languages. By recognizing these nuances, we can gain a more comprehensive understanding of why we express and perceive love the way we do.

Ultimately, the goal of this book is to empower you, the reader, with the knowledge and tools to enhance your relationships. Whether you're seeking to strengthen your romantic partnership, build stronger connections with family members, or foster deeper friendships, the insights gained from understanding love languages can be transformative.

As we delve into the subsequent chapters, we'll journey through each love language individually, delving into their core principles and exploring practical ways to incorporate them into your relationships. By the end of this book, it is my hope that you'll emerge with a newfound appreciation for the diverse ways love can be expressed and received, and a greater capacity to create lasting and meaningful connections with those who matter most.

INTRODUCTION TO LOVE LANGUAGES

Note: This is a summary of the detailed introduction to Love Languages. If you would like more specific details or sections, feel free to ask.

2

The Five Love Languages Unveiled

In this chapter, we will embark on a comprehensive exploration of the five love languages, delving into the core principles of each and gaining a deeper understanding of how they shape the dynamics of relationships. By the end of this chapter, you will have the tools to identify your primary and secondary love languages, setting the stage for more effective communication and connection with your loved ones.

Words of Affirmation: At the heart of this love language lies the power of spoken or written words to uplift and validate. Individuals with Words of Affirmation as their primary love language thrive on hearing verbal expressions of love, appreciation, and encouragement. Simple statements like "I love you," "You mean the world to me," or "I'm proud of you" carry immense weight and significance for them.

Acts of Service: This love language revolves around actions that demonstrate care and thoughtfulness. Individuals who resonate with Acts of Service appreciate gestures that go beyond words, such as helping with chores, cooking a meal, or running errands. These tangible acts represent a way of saying "I love you" through actions rather than words.

Receiving Gifts: For those with Receiving Gifts as their primary love language, the act of giving and receiving gifts is a symbol of love and thoughtfulness. These gifts need not be extravagant; it's the thought behind them that matters most. The effort put into selecting a meaningful gift speaks volumes to these individuals.

Quality Time: Quality Time enthusiasts value undivided attention and meaningful experiences spent together. This love language is all about creating shared memories, engaging in deep conversations, and feeling a genuine connection. Putting away distractions and being fully present are key components of expressing love in this way.

Physical Touch: Physical touch is the language of love for individuals who resonate with this love language. From hugs and kisses to holding hands and cuddling, physical touch is a powerful way to convey affection and emotional closeness. Even small gestures of touch can have a profound impact on these individuals.

Identifying Your Love Languages: Understanding your primary and secondary love languages is a crucial step toward enhancing your relationships. Reflect on how you express affection and what gestures from others make you feel most loved. Consider what actions or words deeply resonate with you. This self-awareness will not only help you communicate your needs to your loved ones but also enable you to better understand their preferences.

Throughout this chapter, we will explore anecdotes, scenarios, and practical exercises to help you uncover your own love languages and those of the people close to you. Keep in mind that your love languages may evolve over time due to life experiences, personal growth, and changing circumstances.

As we delve into the subsequent chapters, armed with this newfound knowledge of the five love languages, we will further examine how these languages can be incorporated into different relationships and scenarios. By cultivating a deeper understanding of love languages, you'll be better equipped to navigate the complex landscape of human connections and foster bonds that are rich in love, understanding, and harmony.

Note: This is a summary of the detailed chapter on The Five Love Languages Unveiled. If you would like more specific details or sections, feel free to ask.

3

Acts of Service: Expressing Love Through Actions

In this chapter, we dive into the love language of Acts of Service, exploring how actions can speak louder than words when it comes to expressing love and care. Acts of Service enthusiasts find deep meaning in actions that cater to their partner's needs and enhance their lives. By understanding this love language, you can forge stronger connections and create a fulfilling bond with your loved ones.

Understanding Acts of Service:

Acts of Service is rooted in the idea that actions have the power to convey love, commitment, and devotion. For individuals with this love language, the phrase "actions speak louder than words" holds true. It's not just about completing tasks; it's about the intention behind those tasks, the effort put forth, and the idea that their partner is willing to invest time and energy to make their life better.

Expressing Love Through Acts of Service:
1. Know Their Needs: To effectively utilize Acts of Service, you must

understand your partner's needs and desires. Pay attention to their daily routines, responsibilities, and preferences. By doing so, you can identify areas where your assistance or efforts would be most appreciated.

2. Small Gestures, Big Impact: Sometimes, it's the small things that matter most. Preparing breakfast, making the bed, or running errands can make a significant difference in your partner's day. These seemingly mundane tasks communicate thoughtfulness and care.

3. Shared Responsibilities: Collaborate on household tasks and responsibilities. When both partners contribute to chores and tasks, it fosters a sense of teamwork and shared commitment to maintaining the relationship.

4. Surprise Acts: Surprise your partner with acts of service they may not expect. It could be cooking their favorite meal after a long day, offering a massage, or organizing a space they use frequently.

5. Communication: Discuss with your partner to understand which acts of service mean the most to them. Open communication helps prevent assumptions and ensures that your efforts align with their preferences.

Challenges and Considerations:
　While Acts of Service can be a beautiful way to express love, it's important to strike a balance and ensure that both partners feel valued and appreciated. Also, be cautious not to take on too much and risk burnout. The intent is to create a mutually beneficial dynamic where both partners contribute and support each other.

Acts of Service in Different Relationships:
　The love language of Acts of Service isn't limited to romantic partnerships. It can also play a significant role in friendships, familial relationships, and even the workplace. The key is understanding the needs and preferences of the people around you and finding ways to support them through your

actions.

Conclusion:

Acts of Service is a powerful love language that has the potential to deepen connections and nurture relationships. By recognizing the significance of actions in expressing love, you can enhance your ability to support and care for your partner in meaningful ways. Through empathy, active listening, and a willingness to serve, you can create a lasting bond that's built on a foundation of genuine care and consideration.

Note: This is a summary of the detailed chapter on Acts of Service as a love language. If you would like more specific details or sections, feel free to ask.

4

Words of Affirmation: The Power of Positive Words

In this chapter, we delve into the love language of Words of Affirmation, exploring the profound impact that positive and meaningful words can have on relationships. Through understanding this love language, you can harness the power of language to uplift, support, and strengthen your connections with loved ones.

The Impact of Words of Affirmation:
Words are potent instruments that can shape emotions and perceptions. For individuals with Words of Affirmation as their love language, verbal expressions of love, appreciation, and encouragement are like nourishment for their emotional well-being. These words serve as a tangible reminder of their worth, fostering a sense of security and validation.

Effective Communication Techniques:
1. Express Love: Verbalize your love explicitly. Use phrases like "I love you," "You mean the world to me," and "I'm grateful for you." These declarations reinforce the depth of your feelings and provide reassurance.

2. Specific Compliments: Be specific in your compliments. Instead of a generic "You're great," offer praise tailored to their qualities or actions. For instance, "I admire your resilience" or "Your creativity inspires me."

3. Appreciation: Regularly express appreciation for their presence in your life. Acknowledge the positive impact they've had on you and the relationship.

4. Encouragement: Provide words of encouragement when your loved one faces challenges. Offer support and remind them of their strengths. Encouragement during difficult times can be a powerful source of motivation.

5. Active Listening: Engage in active listening and respond with empathy. Show that you value their thoughts and feelings by affirming their experiences.

6. Love Notes: Leave surprise love notes in unexpected places. A heartfelt note on the bathroom mirror or tucked into their bag can brighten their day.

7. Public Praise: Don't shy away from expressing your admiration for them in front of others. Public affirmation can amplify the impact of your words.

Challenges and Considerations:
   While Words of Affirmation are a beautiful way to express love, sincerity is key. Empty or insincere words can have the opposite effect, leading to doubt and mistrust. Authenticity in your expressions is crucial for maintaining the integrity of this love language.

Words of Affirmation in Different Relationships:
   The love language of Words of Affirmation isn't limited to romantic relationships. It can be a powerful tool in nurturing connections with friends, family members, and colleagues. Everyone benefits from knowing they are valued and appreciated.

Conclusion:

Words possess the remarkable ability to create bonds, instill confidence, and build emotional bridges. By mastering the art of verbal affirmation, you can cultivate a relationship enriched with positivity and understanding. The language you use becomes a conduit for affection, validation, and encouragement, strengthening the foundation of your connections and enhancing your overall emotional intimacy.

Note: This is a summary of the detailed chapter on Words of Affirmation as a love language. If you would like more specific details or sections, feel free to ask.

5

Receiving Gifts: Symbolic Expressions of Love

In this chapter, we explore the love language of Receiving Gifts, delving into the profound significance of giving and receiving meaningful presents as a way of expressing love. By understanding the nuances of this love language, you can foster deeper connections and create lasting memories through thoughtful gestures.

The Meaning Behind Receiving Gifts:
For individuals who identify with the love language of Receiving Gifts, the act of giving and receiving presents goes beyond materialism. These gifts symbolize thoughtfulness, intention, and the effort to understand their preferences and desires. Such gestures provide tangible evidence of love, making them feel cherished and valued.

Strategies for Meaningful Gift Giving and Receiving:
1. Thoughtful Selection: Pay attention to your loved one's interests, hobbies, and desires. Thoughtful gifts show that you have taken the time to understand their preferences.

2. Sentimental Value: Opt for gifts that carry sentimental value. Personalized items, keepsakes, or items that remind them of shared memories can be incredibly meaningful.

3. Quality Over Quantity: It's not about the monetary value of the gift, but the emotional value it holds. Focus on the quality and thoughtfulness of the present rather than its price tag.

4. Occasions and Surprises: While special occasions are opportunities for gift giving, surprises can be equally impactful. Unexpected gifts can brighten someone's day and reinforce your affection.

5. Emotional Presentation: The way you present the gift matters. Take the time to create an environment of anticipation and excitement around the exchange.

6. Receiving Gracefully: If Receiving Gifts is your loved one's primary love language, graciously accept the gifts they give you. Understand that their intention is to express love, not solely to impress or outdo others.

Challenges and Considerations:
   When expressing love through gifts, it's important to strike a balance. Overemphasis on the material aspect of the gift can overshadow the emotional connection. It's also crucial to understand that not everyone values gifts in the same way, so open communication is key to ensuring that both partners feel understood and appreciated.

Receiving Gifts in Different Relationships:
   The love language of Receiving Gifts can extend to various relationships beyond romantic ones. Friends, family members, and colleagues can also benefit from the positive impact of thoughtful gift-giving.

Conclusion:

RECEIVING GIFTS: SYMBOLIC EXPRESSIONS OF LOVE

Receiving Gifts is a love language that transcends materialism and taps into the emotional realm. Through meaningful gestures, you can communicate your understanding, appreciation, and love for your partner. The effort you put into selecting and giving presents reflects your commitment to fostering a deep and meaningful connection. When approached with sincerity and care, this love language can transform routine moments into cherished memories.

Note: This is a summary of the detailed chapter on Receiving Gifts as a love language. If you would like more specific details or sections, feel free to ask.

6

Quality Time: The Value of Undivided Attention

In this chapter, we delve into the love language of Quality Time, exploring the profound significance of spending meaningful moments together in relationships. By understanding the depth of this love language, you can foster genuine connections and create lasting memories that nurture your bonds.

The Importance of Quality Time:

Quality Time is more than mere companionship; it's about creating undistracted, focused moments that allow for genuine connection and emotional intimacy. For individuals with Quality Time as their love language, nothing says "I love you" more than the gift of your undivided attention.

Techniques for Creating Meaningful Connections:

1. Be Present: Put away distractions such as phones, laptops, and other devices when spending time together. Show that you are fully engaged and attentive to your partner.

QUALITY TIME: THE VALUE OF UNDIVIDED ATTENTION

2. Listen Actively: Engage in active listening during conversations. Give your partner space to express themselves, and respond with genuine interest and empathy.

3. Plan Quality Activities: Plan activities that align with your partner's interests. Whether it's hiking, cooking, or watching a movie, the key is to engage in activities that foster interaction and connection.

4. Share Experiences: Participate in experiences that allow you to learn, grow, and have shared stories. Trying new things together can create lasting memories.

5. Scheduled Time: Set aside dedicated time for one-on-one interaction. Whether it's a weekly date night or a weekend getaway, carving out time specifically for each other is essential.

6. Physical Presence: Physical presence is as important as mental presence. Holding hands, hugging, and cuddling can enhance the emotional connection during quality time.

7. Ask Open-Ended Questions: Pose open-ended questions that encourage deeper conversations. This can lead to discussions about dreams, values, and aspirations.

Challenges and Considerations:
While Quality Time can be incredibly rewarding, it requires intentional effort. Balancing busy schedules and commitments can sometimes be a challenge. It's important to communicate your dedication to spending quality time and finding ways to prioritize it in your relationship.

Quality Time in Different Relationships:
The love language of Quality Time extends beyond romantic partnerships. Spending meaningful time with family members, friends, and even colleagues

can strengthen connections and enhance overall satisfaction in those relationships.

Conclusion:

Quality Time is a love language that speaks volumes about your commitment and willingness to invest in the relationship. Through shared moments, conversations, and experiences, you can create a deep sense of connection that goes beyond superficial interactions. By understanding the importance of quality time, you can cultivate a bond that is built on mutual understanding, trust, and emotional closeness.

Note: This is a summary of the detailed chapter on Quality Time as a love language. If you would like more specific details or sections, feel free to ask.

7

Physical Touch: The Language of Physical Connection

In this chapter, we explore the love language of Physical Touch, delving into the profound significance of physical connection as a way of expressing love. By understanding the depth of this love language, you can foster a deeper level of intimacy and create a strong emotional bond with your loved ones.

The Role of Physical Touch in Expressing Love:
  Physical touch is a powerful means of communication that transcends words. For individuals with Physical Touch as their love language, physical contact provides a tangible affirmation of love and affection. From hugs and kisses to holding hands and cuddling, these gestures are a way to feel emotionally connected and secure.

Strategies for Enhancing Physical Intimacy:
  1. Consistent Affection: Consistently incorporate physical touch into your interactions. Simple gestures like holding hands, hugging, and gentle touches on the arm can communicate love and care.

2. Non-Sexual Physical Contact: Recognize that physical touch isn't limited to sexual intimacy. Incorporate non-sexual touch throughout your day-to-day interactions to create a continuous sense of closeness.

3. Intimate Moments: Set aside intentional moments for more intimate physical connection. Cuddling, back rubs, and massages can deepen your emotional bond.

4. Physical Presence: Sit close, lean in, and maintain physical proximity. Being physically close sends a message of interest and availability for emotional connection.

5. Comforting Gestures: Use physical touch to provide comfort and reassurance during difficult times. A hug or a reassuring hand on the shoulder can offer immense support.

6. Communication: Discuss your preferences with your partner. Be open about what types of physical touch are most meaningful to you and how they can incorporate them into your relationship.

Challenges and Considerations:
It's important to respect boundaries and comfort levels when it comes to physical touch. Not everyone is equally receptive to certain types of touch, and it's crucial to communicate openly and ensure that both partners feel comfortable and respected.

Physical Touch in Different Relationships:
Physical Touch is a love language that extends to various relationships. Platonic friendships, familial bonds, and even professional connections can benefit from appropriate and meaningful physical touch.

Conclusion:
Physical Touch is a love language that carries the power to foster emotional

connection and security. By understanding its significance and incorporating physical touch into your interactions, you can create a relationship that is rich in emotional depth and mutual affection. Through gestures that range from the simplest touch to the most intimate embrace, you can communicate love, closeness, and a sense of belonging that words alone can't convey.

Note: This is a summary of the detailed chapter on Physical Touch as a love language. If you would like more specific details or sections, feel free to ask.

8

Discovering Your Partner's Love Language

In this chapter, we delve into the process of identifying your partner's primary love language, equipping you with the tools to understand their preferences and cater to their emotional needs. By uncovering their love language, you can strengthen your relationship by expressing love in ways that resonate deeply with them.

Techniques for Identifying Your Partner's Love Language:

1. Observation: Pay close attention to how your partner expresses love to you and others. Their natural inclinations might reflect their own love language.

2. Communication: Engage in open and honest conversations about love languages. Ask questions about what makes them feel most loved and valued.

3. Gift of Choice: Consider gifting them the book "The Five Love Languages" by Dr. Gary Chapman or taking online quizzes together to identify each other's love languages.

4. Reflect on Their Expressions: Reflect on past experiences and interactions.

DISCOVERING YOUR PARTNER'S LOVE LANGUAGE

What gestures or actions have evoked the most positive response from them?

5. Experiment: Try expressing love in different ways and observe their reactions. Over time, patterns may emerge that provide insight into their love language.

Benefits of Understanding and Catering to Their Language:
   1. Deeper Connection: When you communicate love in a way that aligns with your partner's love language, you create a deeper emotional connection that fosters intimacy and understanding.

2. Enhanced Communication: Understanding their love language allows you to communicate more effectively and resolve conflicts with greater empathy.

3. Reduced Misunderstandings: By knowing their preferences, you can avoid unintentional misinterpretations of affection and ensure that your efforts are well-received.

4. Lasting Impact: Expressing love in your partner's love language has a lasting impact, helping them feel consistently valued and cherished.

5. Relationship Growth: Catering to their love language encourages personal growth and mutual effort in making the relationship thrive.

Cultivating a Love Language-Centric Relationship:
   1. Practice Patience: Learning and adapting to each other's love languages takes time and patience. Be open to the process.

2. Mutual Understanding: Both partners should make an effort to understand each other's love languages, creating a reciprocal cycle of love and appreciation.

3. Consistent Effort: Regularly express love in ways that align with their love

language. Consistency reinforces the emotional connection.

4. Flexibility: Love languages can evolve over time. Be attuned to changes in preferences due to life experiences and growth.

Conclusion:

Discovering and catering to your partner's love language is an investment in the emotional well-being of your relationship. By taking the time to understand their preferences, you pave the way for a relationship that is built on mutual understanding, respect, and a deep sense of connection. As you speak their love language fluently, you create a bond that is resilient, fulfilling, and rich in affection.

Note: This is a summary of the detailed chapter on Discovering Your Partner's Love Language. If you would like more specific details or sections, feel free to ask.

9

Navigating Relationships with Different Love Languages

In this chapter, we explore the complexities of relationships when partners have differing love languages. We'll delve into strategies that can help bridge gaps, enhance communication, and foster understanding between individuals who express and receive love in distinct ways.

Navigating Differences in Love Languages:

1. Awareness: Recognize that people have unique ways of feeling loved. Understand that your partner's love language isn't a rejection of your efforts but a reflection of their emotional needs.

2. Open Communication: Have open conversations about your love languages. Share your preferences, express your needs, and listen actively to your partner's perspective.

3. Appreciate Diversity: Embrace the diversity of love languages. Just as people have varied personalities, love languages also contribute to what makes each person unique.

Strategies for Meeting Each Other's Needs:

1. Compromise: Find a middle ground by incorporating elements of both partners' love languages into your relationship. This may involve making small adjustments in how you express affection.

2. Quality Time and Physical Touch: If one partner's love language is Quality Time and the other's is Physical Touch, combining activities like cuddling while watching a movie can meet both needs.

3. Words of Affirmation and Acts of Service: If one partner's love language is Words of Affirmation and the other's is Acts of Service, expressing appreciation verbally while helping with tasks can create a balanced dynamic.

4. Receiving Gifts and Quality Time: If one partner's love language is Receiving Gifts and the other's is Quality Time, planning special experiences together can blend both languages.

5. Understanding Love in Action: Remember that love languages reflect how someone expresses love, not the depth of their feelings. A partner who prefers Acts of Service may still deeply care for their Quality Time-loving partner.

Building Bridges Between Love Languages:

1. Curiosity: Show genuine interest in your partner's love language. Ask questions, listen attentively, and seek to understand the emotional significance behind their preferences.

2. Flexibility: Be flexible in adapting to your partner's love language, even if it's not your own. Embrace the opportunity to grow and learn through their perspective.

3. Collaboration: Collaborate on ways to express love that resonate with both partners. Experiment with new ways of connecting that incorporate elements from each love language.

4. Empathy: Put yourself in your partner's shoes and imagine how their love language fulfills their emotional needs. This can help you appreciate their viewpoint and efforts.

Conclusion:

Navigating relationships with different love languages requires effort, patience, and a commitment to understanding and growth. By acknowledging and respecting each other's preferences, you can create a harmonious partnership where both partners feel loved, valued, and cherished. The journey of bridging gaps and connecting across love languages enriches the relationship with depth, intimacy, and lasting joy.

Note: This is a summary of the detailed chapter on Navigating Relationships with Different Love Languages. If you would like more specific details or sections, feel free to ask.

10

Applying Love Languages in Daily Life

In this final chapter, we delve into the practical application of love languages in your daily interactions. We'll explore how to seamlessly integrate each love language into your relationship, creating a more fulfilling and harmonious connection that enriches both partners' lives.

Integrating Love Languages into Everyday Interactions:

1. Morning Rituals: Start the day with a loving gesture that aligns with your partner's love language. It could be a warm hug, a heartfelt compliment, or a cup of their favorite morning beverage.

2. Texts and Notes: Send surprise texts or leave handwritten notes that cater to your partner's love language. Words of Affirmation lovers can receive daily compliments, while Acts of Service enthusiasts might appreciate a reminder of how much you value their help.

3. Shared Activities: Plan activities that cater to each other's love languages. A picnic in the park for Quality Time lovers or a surprise homemade meal for Acts of Service lovers can create memorable moments.

4. Embracing Hobbies: Get involved in each other's hobbies to express support and interest. Join your partner in a dance class (Physical Touch) or help them organize their workspace (Acts of Service).

5. Celebration Days: Celebrate special occasions by incorporating each other's love languages. A heartfelt letter for Words of Affirmation lovers or a well-thought-out gift for Receiving Gifts enthusiasts can make the day memorable.

Creative Ways to Incorporate Love Languages:
   1. Theme Nights: Dedicate a night to each love language. Have a "Cooking Together" night for Acts of Service, or a "Movie Marathon" night for Quality Time.

2. Memory Jar: Create a jar filled with notes that represent each love language. Each week, pick a note and fulfill the request written on it.

3. Surprise Adventure: Plan a surprise adventure that incorporates all five love languages. This could involve exploring a new place, sharing quality time, exchanging small gifts, offering words of affirmation, and engaging in physical touch.

4. Language Exchange: Teach each other phrases in a foreign language, adding a layer of creativity to your expressions of love.

5. Dream Board: Collaborate on a dream board that reflects each partner's aspirations. This melds Quality Time with Acts of Service and Words of Affirmation.

Sustaining the Momentum:
   1. Regular Check-ins: Periodically review how well you're integrating each other's love languages. Adjust and adapt as your relationship evolves.

2. Celebrate Efforts: Acknowledge each other's efforts in applying love languages. Regularly express gratitude for the thought and care invested in making the relationship flourish.

3. Reflect and Grow: Reflect on how applying love languages has enhanced your relationship. Consider ways to further deepen your connection.

Conclusion:

Applying love languages in daily life transforms your relationship into a canvas of affection, appreciation, and understanding. By embracing each other's preferences and intentionally expressing love in ways that resonate, you create a vibrant and thriving bond. The journey of incorporating love languages into your relationship is a lifelong process of growth, connection, and shared happiness.

Note: This is a summary of the detailed chapter on Applying Love Languages in Daily Life. If you would like more specific details or sections, feel free to ask.

11

Enhancing Intimacy Through Love Languages

In this chapter, we explore how love languages can serve as a powerful catalyst for deepening both emotional and physical intimacy in your relationship. By harnessing the unique strengths of each love language, you can enhance the connection between you and your partner, fostering a bond that is rich in both depth and passion.

Deepening Emotional Intimacy:

1. Vulnerability: Expressing your love language requires vulnerability. By opening up and sharing your needs, desires, and emotions, you create a safe space for emotional intimacy to flourish.

2. Active Listening: Pay attention to your partner's expressions of love. When they speak their love language, actively listen and respond with empathy, showing that you understand and care deeply.

3. Shared Experiences: Participate in activities that align with both partners' love languages. These shared experiences create memories that contribute to

a shared emotional history.

4. Empathy and Validation: Catering to your partner's love language demonstrates empathy and validation, key ingredients for emotional intimacy.

Enhancing Physical Intimacy:
1. Physical Touch and Passion: For those with Physical Touch as their love language, affectionate gestures outside the bedroom can foster a sense of closeness that naturally translates into increased physical intimacy.

2. Quality Time and Connection: Spending quality time together outside the bedroom can enhance emotional connection, which in turn deepens physical intimacy. Emotional closeness often leads to a more fulfilling physical relationship.

3. Acts of Service and Comfort: Acts of Service can contribute to a sense of comfort and safety in the relationship, making partners more inclined to open up emotionally and physically.

4. Words of Affirmation and Confidence: Words of Affirmation can boost confidence and self-esteem, positively impacting one's willingness to be vulnerable and explore physical intimacy.

Techniques for Enhancing Connection:
1. Love Language Exchanges: Periodically switch roles and express love in your partner's primary love language. This practice deepens your understanding of their experience and fosters reciprocity.

2. Intimate Surprises: Surprise your partner with gestures that cater to their love language, fostering a sense of anticipation and excitement that enhances intimacy.

3. Non-Verbal Cues: Develop non-verbal cues that communicate affection in

each other's love languages. These cues can create moments of connection even in busy or public settings.

4. Reflective Conversations: Engage in reflective conversations about how your love languages impact both emotional and physical intimacy. Sharing insights can lead to mutual understanding and growth.

Conclusion:

By embracing and applying love languages, you can transform your relationship into a harmonious blend of emotional and physical intimacy. The synergy of catering to each other's unique preferences creates a space where love, connection, and passion coexist. As you deepen your emotional understanding and physical connection through the language of love, you foster an enduring bond that withstands the test of time.

Note: This is a summary of the detailed chapter on Enhancing Intimacy Through Love Languages. If you would like more specific details or sections, feel free to ask.

12

The Journey of Love Languages

In this final chapter, we embark on a reflective journey, exploring the profound impact of understanding and embracing love languages in your relationship. We'll delve into the ongoing practice of love languages and how they contribute to the growth and nurturing of your connection.

Reflecting on the Impact:
1. Transformational Insights: Reflect on how discovering your love languages and those of your partner has transformed your relationship. Consider the newfound depth of understanding and connection you've achieved.

2. Communication Breakthroughs: Recall instances where applying love languages led to breakthroughs in communication and conflict resolution. Acknowledge the positive impact this had on your relationship.

3. Shared Memories: Reflect on the shared memories and experiences that were created by incorporating each other's love languages into your interactions.

Nurturing a Relationship Through Ongoing Practice:

1. Continual Learning: Recognize that the journey of understanding love languages is ongoing. As individuals evolve, so can their preferences and needs.

2. Flexibility and Adaptation: Embrace the need for flexibility and adaptation as you continue to apply love languages. As life circumstances change, your strategies for expressing love may need adjustment.

3. Strengthening Bonds: Use love languages as a tool to strengthen bonds during challenging times. The application of love languages can provide comfort, stability, and a source of reassurance.

4. Celebrating Progress: Celebrate the milestones achieved through applying love languages. Acknowledge the growth and progress in your relationship's emotional and physical intimacy.

Fostering Growth and Connection:

1. Shared Goals: Set shared goals for how you intend to continue integrating love languages into your relationship. This shared commitment ensures ongoing growth.

2. Communication Tune-Ups: Regularly engage in open conversations about your love languages. Revisit your understanding of each other's needs and preferences.

3. Surprises and Special Moments: Infuse your relationship with surprises and special moments that cater to each other's love languages. These moments help keep the spark alive.

4. Learning from Challenges: Use challenges as opportunities to apply love languages to problem-solving and conflict resolution. Addressing challenges in a language that resonates with each partner can lead to solutions that

strengthen your bond.

Summary:

The journey of love languages is one of continuous growth, discovery, and renewal. By embracing each other's unique preferences and consistently applying love languages, you create a relationship that thrives on mutual understanding, empathy, and connection. As you navigate the twists and turns of life, remember that the language of love is a powerful tool that can guide you toward enduring happiness, intimacy, and a love that flourishes through all seasons.

Note: This is a summary of the detailed chapter on The Journey of Love Languages. If you would like more specific details or sections, feel free to ask.

Conclusion: Understanding Love Languages

The journey of understanding love languages has been one of profound self-discovery, empathy, and connection. In exploring the intricacies of how individuals express and receive love, we've uncovered a roadmap that leads to deeper emotional intimacy, stronger relationships, and lasting fulfillment. Through the exploration of five distinct love languages—Acts of Service, Words of Affirmation, Receiving Gifts, Quality Time, and Physical Touch—we've gained insights into the diverse ways people interpret and communicate love.

Our exploration has illuminated the fact that love is not a one-size-fits-all concept. Instead, it's a dynamic and multifaceted phenomenon that requires attentive listening, open communication, and a willingness to adapt. Understanding and embracing each other's love languages has the potential to bridge gaps, dissolve misunderstandings, and foster an environment of mutual appreciation.

As we conclude our journey of understanding love languages, remember that the application of this knowledge is an ongoing process. It's not just about knowing your own love language or that of your partner—it's about actively integrating these insights into your daily interactions. By making a conscious effort to speak your partner's love language, you create a language of love that resonates deeply and transcends words.

Through acts of service, heartfelt affirmations, thoughtful gifts, quality time, and physical touch, you've embarked on a path of growth and connection. The language of love, as expressed through these love languages, has the power to mend, enrich, and rejuvenate relationships. By committing to nurturing and understanding your partner in the ways they most deeply appreciate, you've embarked on a journey of love that has the potential to flourish indefinitely.

In your quest for a love that thrives, remember that you hold the key to unlocking a connection that is genuine, harmonious, and enduring. With the knowledge of love languages at your disposal, you possess the ability to create a symphony of affection, understanding, and deep emotional resonance. As you move forward, may your relationships be forever enriched by the beauty of love languages, and may your journey be one of continuous growth, mutual admiration, and love that knows no bounds.

www.ingramcontent.com/pod-product-compliance
Lightning Source LLC
LaVergne TN
LVHW010441070526
838199LV00066B/6121